FRACTIONS MADE EASY MATH ESSENTIALS

Children's Fraction Books

All Rights reserved. No part of this book may be reproduced or used in any way or form or by any means whether electronic or mechanical, this means that you cannot record or photocopy any material ideas or tips that are provided in this book.

Copyright 2016

Enjoy and have fun with Fraction Exercises.

Set 1

Write the fraction of the shaded area.

1. 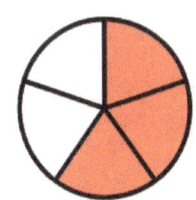 _____

2. 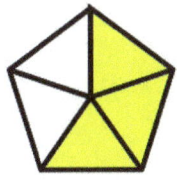 _____

3.  _____

4. 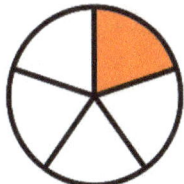 _____

5. 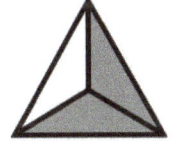 _____

6. 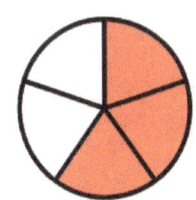 _____

7.  _____

8. 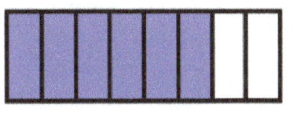 _____

9.  _____

10. 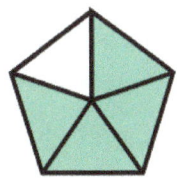 _____

11.  _____

12. 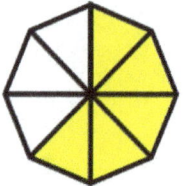 _____

13.  _____

14. 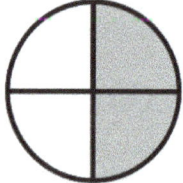 _____

15.  _____

16. 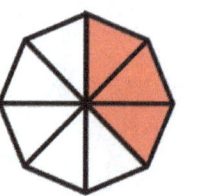 _____

17.  _____

18. 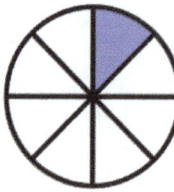 _____

19.  _____

20. 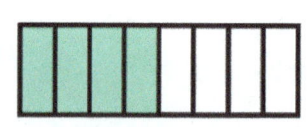 _____

21. 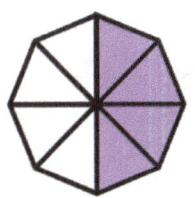 26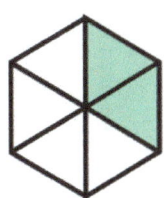

_____ _____

22.  27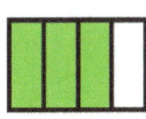

_____ _____

23.  28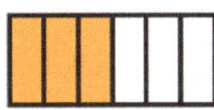

_____ _____

24. 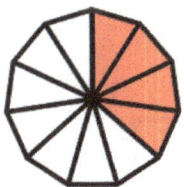 29

_____ _____

25. 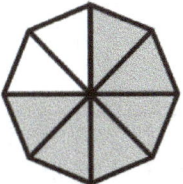 30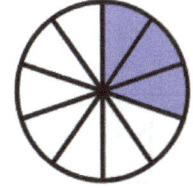

_____ _____

31. 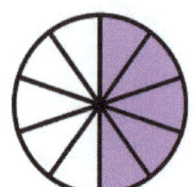 _____

32. 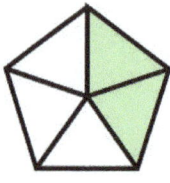 _____

33.  _____

34. 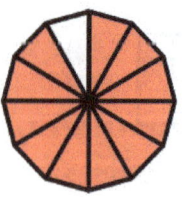 _____

35.  _____

36. 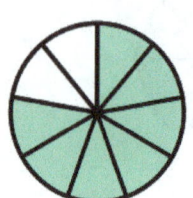 _____

37.  _____

38. 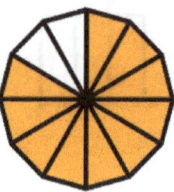 _____

39. 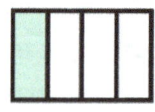 _____

40.  _____

Set 2

Write the fraction of the shaded area.

1. 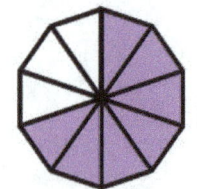 _____

2. 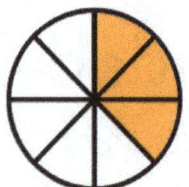 _____

3. 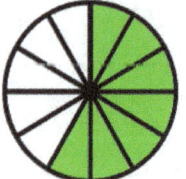 _____

4.  _____

5.  _____

6. 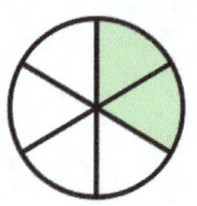 _____

7.  _____

8.  _____

9.  _____

10. 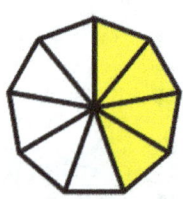 _____

11. 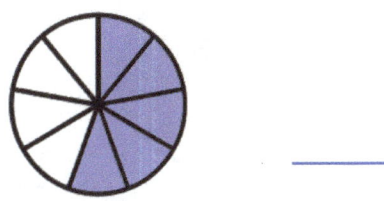 _____

16. 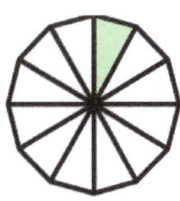 _____

12. 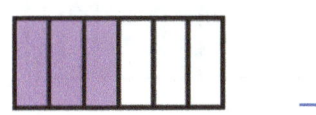 _____

17. 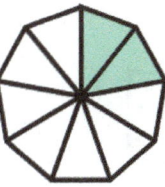 _____

13. 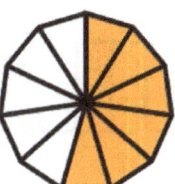 _____

18. 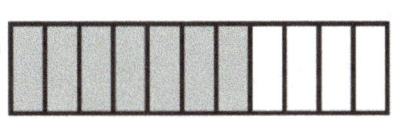 _____

14.  _____

19.  _____

15.  _____

20.  _____

21. 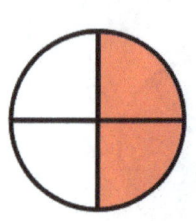 _____

22.  _____

23.  _____

24. 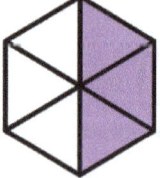 _____

25.  _____

26. 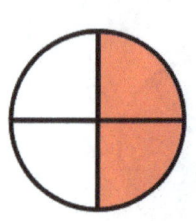 _____

27. 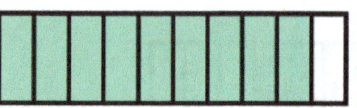 _____

28.  _____

29. 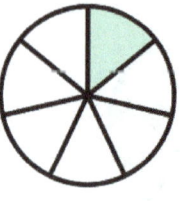 _____

30. 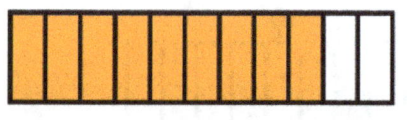 _____

31.  _____

32. 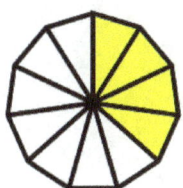 _____

33. 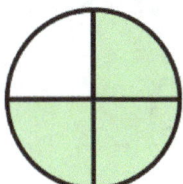 _____

34. 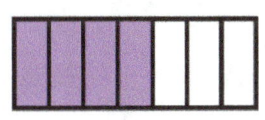 _____

35.  _____

36. 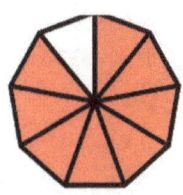 _____

37.  _____

38. 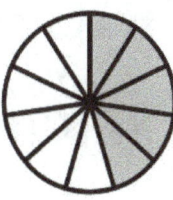 _____

39.  _____

40. 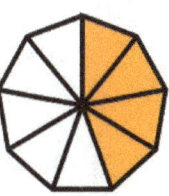 _____

Set 3

Shade the pie with the indicated fraction

1.  $\dfrac{2}{3}$ _____

2.  $\dfrac{2}{5}$ _____

3.  $\dfrac{1}{5}$ _____

4.  $\dfrac{1}{6}$ _____

5.  $\dfrac{4}{6}$ _____

6.  $\dfrac{4}{7}$ _____

7. 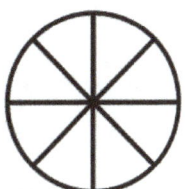 $\dfrac{3}{8}$ _____

8.  $\dfrac{3}{5}$ _____

9.  $\dfrac{1}{3}$ _____

10.  $\dfrac{7}{8}$ _____

11. 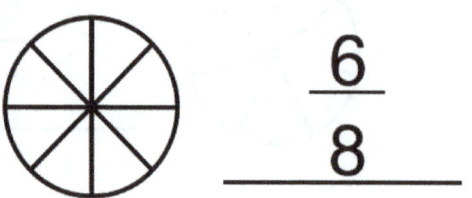 $\dfrac{6}{8}$

16. 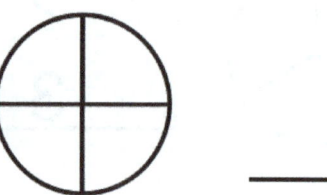 $\dfrac{2}{4}$

12. 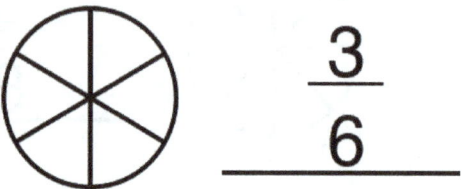 $\dfrac{3}{6}$

17.  $\dfrac{6}{7}$

13. 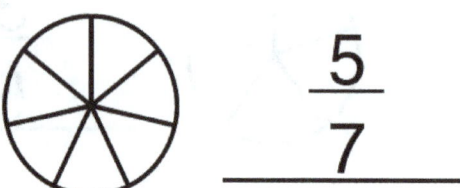 $\dfrac{5}{7}$

18. 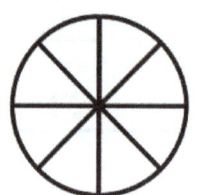 $\dfrac{4}{8}$

14. 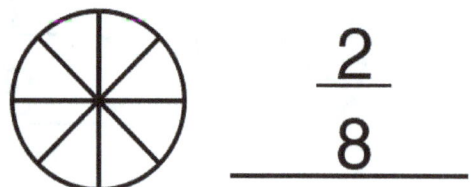 $\dfrac{2}{8}$

19.  $\dfrac{5}{6}$

15. 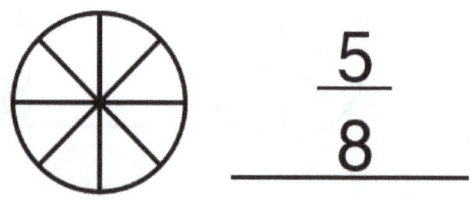 $\dfrac{5}{8}$

20.  $\dfrac{1}{4}$

21. 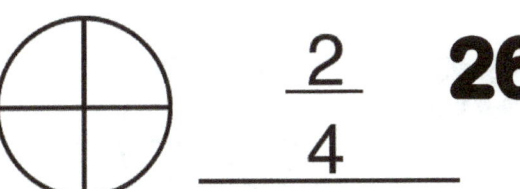 $\frac{2}{4}$ 26.  $\frac{4}{6}$

22. 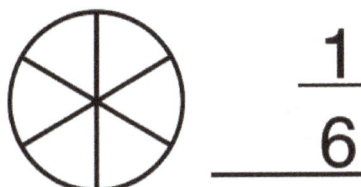 $\frac{1}{6}$ 27. $\frac{1}{8}$

23.  $\frac{4}{7}$ 28. $\frac{1}{7}$

24.  $\frac{1}{4}$ 29.  $\frac{2}{7}$

25.  $\frac{2}{5}$ 30. 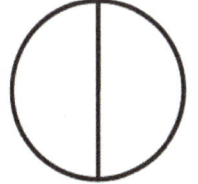 $\frac{1}{2}$

31. 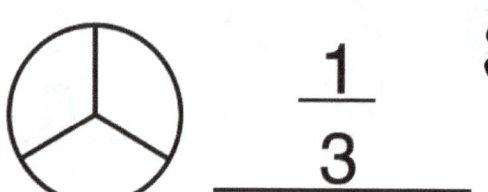 $\dfrac{1}{3}$

36. 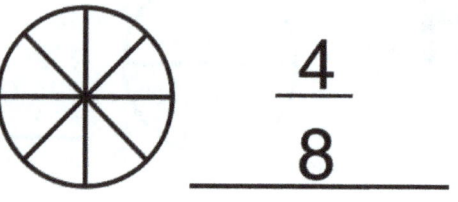 $\dfrac{4}{8}$

32.  $\dfrac{6}{7}$

37.  $\dfrac{3}{5}$

33.  $\dfrac{1}{5}$

38.  $\dfrac{2}{6}$

34.  $\dfrac{3}{6}$

39.  $\dfrac{3}{4}$

35.  $\dfrac{2}{8}$

40.  $\dfrac{6}{8}$

Set 4

Shade the pie with the indicated fraction

1. 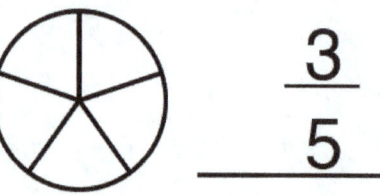 $\dfrac{3}{5}$

2. 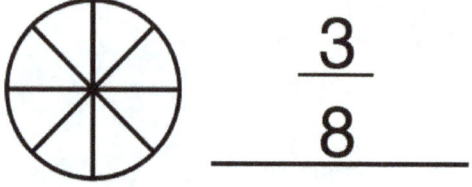 $\dfrac{3}{8}$

3. 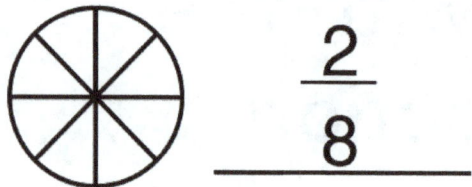 $\dfrac{2}{8}$

4. 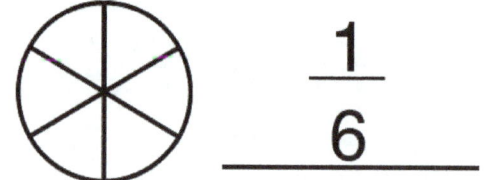 $\dfrac{1}{6}$

5. 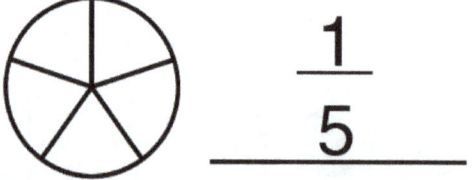 $\dfrac{1}{5}$

6. 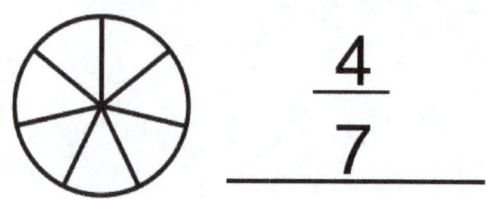 $\dfrac{4}{7}$

7. $\dfrac{1}{3}$

8. 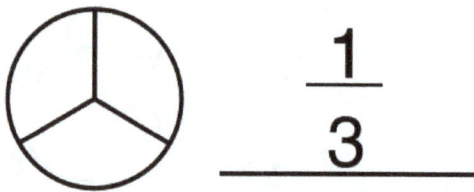 $\dfrac{1}{7}$

9. 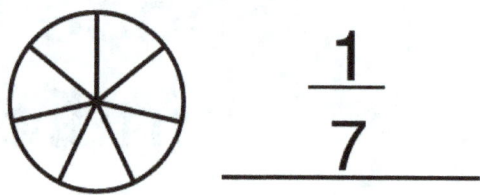 $\dfrac{6}{7}$

10. 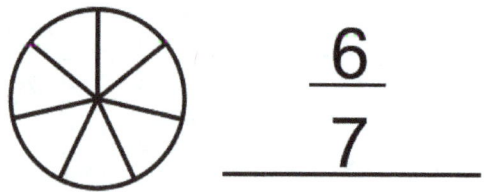 $\dfrac{2}{6}$

11. 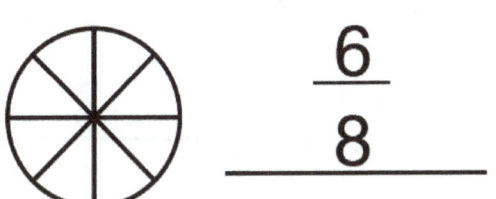 $\dfrac{6}{8}$ _____

12. 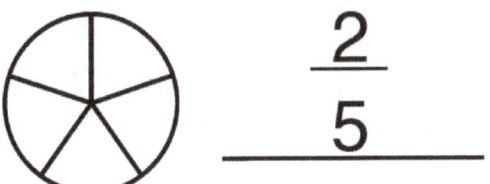 $\dfrac{2}{5}$ _____

13. 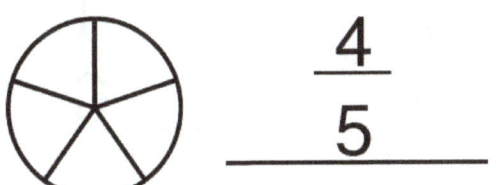 $\dfrac{4}{5}$ _____

14. 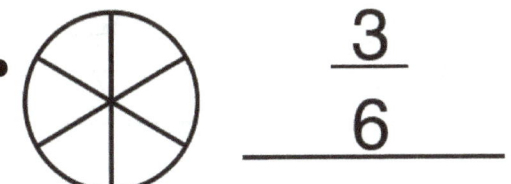 $\dfrac{3}{6}$ _____

15. 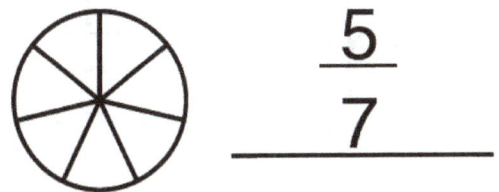 $\dfrac{5}{7}$ _____

16. 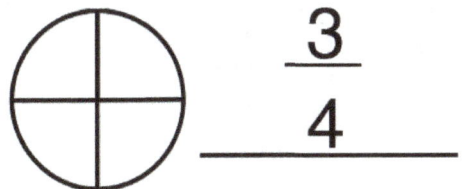 $\dfrac{3}{4}$ _____

17. 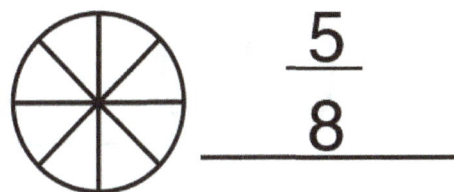 $\dfrac{5}{8}$ _____

18. 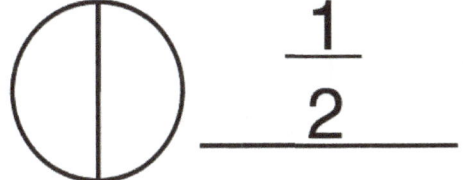 $\dfrac{1}{2}$ _____

19. 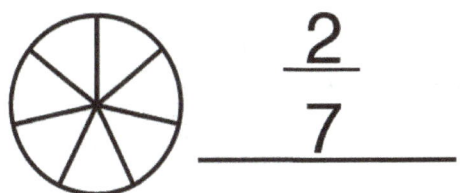 $\dfrac{2}{7}$ _____

20. 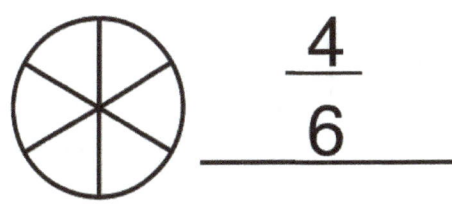 $\dfrac{4}{6}$ _____

21.  $\dfrac{3}{8}$ _____   **26**  $\dfrac{1}{8}$ _____

22.  $\dfrac{1}{3}$ _____   **27**  $\dfrac{1}{2}$ _____

23.  $\dfrac{3}{6}$ _____   **28**  $\dfrac{4}{6}$ _____

24.  $\dfrac{2}{6}$ _____   **29**  $\dfrac{3}{7}$ _____

25.  $\dfrac{7}{8}$ _____   **30** 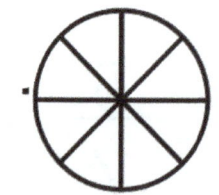 $\dfrac{4}{8}$ _____

31. 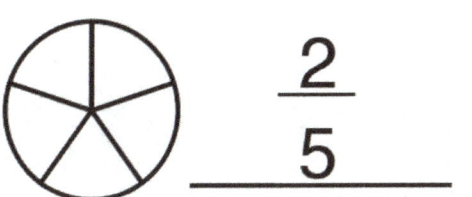 $\dfrac{2}{5}$ _____

32. 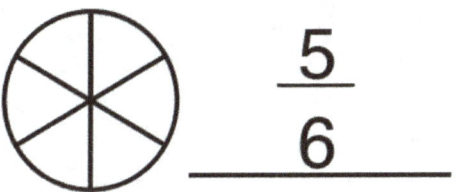 $\dfrac{5}{6}$ _____

33. 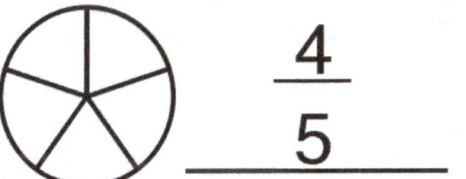 $\dfrac{4}{5}$ _____

34.  $\dfrac{5}{7}$ _____

35. 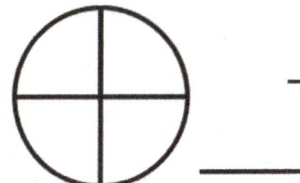 $\dfrac{3}{4}$ _____

36.  $\dfrac{6}{8}$ _____

37.  $\dfrac{6}{7}$ _____

38. 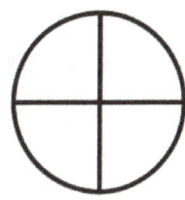 $\dfrac{2}{4}$ _____

39.  $\dfrac{1}{4}$ _____

40.  $\dfrac{2}{3}$ _____

Set 5

Add the fractions.

1. $\dfrac{1}{6} + \dfrac{4}{6} =$

2. $\dfrac{5}{12} + \dfrac{6}{12} =$

3. $\dfrac{3}{11} + \dfrac{7}{11} =$

4. $\dfrac{3}{7} + \dfrac{3}{7} =$

5. $\dfrac{1}{3} + \dfrac{1}{3} =$

6. $\dfrac{1}{5} + \dfrac{2}{5} =$

7. $\dfrac{3}{11} + \dfrac{6}{11} =$

8. $\dfrac{2}{9} + \dfrac{4}{9} =$

9. $\dfrac{3}{10} + \dfrac{6}{10} =$

10. $\dfrac{3}{12} + \dfrac{5}{12} =$

11. $\dfrac{1}{12} + \dfrac{8}{12} =$

12. $\dfrac{2}{9} + \dfrac{3}{9} =$

13. $\dfrac{1}{4} + \dfrac{2}{4} =$

14. $\dfrac{1}{8} + \dfrac{3}{8} =$

15. $\dfrac{1}{4} + \dfrac{1}{4} =$

16. $\dfrac{1}{9} + \dfrac{5}{9} =$

17. $\dfrac{1}{11} + \dfrac{9}{11} =$

18. $\dfrac{1}{3} + \dfrac{1}{3} =$

19. $\dfrac{1}{12} + \dfrac{4}{12} =$

20. $\dfrac{2}{8} + \dfrac{3}{8} =$

21. $\dfrac{1}{6} + \dfrac{2}{6} =$

22. $\dfrac{1}{5} + \dfrac{2}{5} =$

23. $\dfrac{3}{10} + \dfrac{5}{10} =$

24. $\dfrac{1}{9} + \dfrac{7}{9} =$

25. $\dfrac{1}{11} + \dfrac{6}{11} =$

26. $\dfrac{1}{12} + \dfrac{9}{12} =$

27. $\dfrac{1}{10} + \dfrac{3}{10} =$

28. $\dfrac{1}{12} + \dfrac{4}{12} =$

29. $\dfrac{1}{6} + \dfrac{3}{6} =$ _____

30. $\dfrac{2}{10} + \dfrac{3}{10} =$ _____

31. $\dfrac{2}{7} + \dfrac{4}{7} =$ _____

32. $\dfrac{1}{10} + \dfrac{2}{10} =$ _____

33. $\dfrac{1}{12} + \dfrac{8}{12} =$ _____

34. $\dfrac{2}{12} + \dfrac{8}{12} =$ _____

35. $\dfrac{1}{5} + \dfrac{1}{5} =$ _____

36. $\dfrac{3}{12} + \dfrac{4}{12} =$

37. $\dfrac{1}{4} + \dfrac{2}{4} =$

38. $\dfrac{4}{9} + \dfrac{4}{9} =$

39. $\dfrac{4}{11} + \dfrac{4}{11} =$

40. $\dfrac{3}{9} + \dfrac{4}{9} =$

41. $\dfrac{1}{3} + \dfrac{1}{3} =$

42. $\dfrac{1}{11} + \dfrac{8}{11} =$

43. $\dfrac{2}{10} + \dfrac{5}{10} =$

44. $\dfrac{3}{11} + \dfrac{3}{11} =$

45. $\dfrac{2}{9} + \dfrac{2}{9} =$

46. $\dfrac{2}{6} + \dfrac{2}{6} =$

47. $\dfrac{1}{12} + \dfrac{2}{12} =$

48. $\dfrac{1}{3} + \dfrac{1}{3} =$

49. $\dfrac{5}{11} + \dfrac{5}{11} =$

50. $\dfrac{1}{4} + \dfrac{1}{4} =$

51. $\dfrac{1}{7} + \dfrac{5}{7} =$

52. $\dfrac{1}{9} + \dfrac{6}{9} =$

53. $\dfrac{3}{12} + \dfrac{7}{12} =$

54. $\dfrac{1}{12} + \dfrac{5}{12} =$

55. $\dfrac{1}{10} + \dfrac{1}{10} =$

56. $\dfrac{1}{5} + \dfrac{1}{5} =$

Answers

Set 1

1. $\dfrac{2}{5}$
2. $\dfrac{3}{5}$
3. $\dfrac{1}{5}$
4. $\dfrac{2}{3}$
5. $\dfrac{4}{5}$
6. $\dfrac{3}{5}$
7. $\dfrac{2}{8}$
8. $\dfrac{6}{8}$
9. $\dfrac{1}{4}$
10. $\dfrac{4}{5}$
11. $\dfrac{2}{5}$
12. $\dfrac{5}{8}$
13. $\dfrac{3}{4}$
14. $\dfrac{2}{4}$
15. $\dfrac{1}{2}$
16. $\dfrac{3}{8}$
17. $\dfrac{7}{8}$
18. $\dfrac{1}{8}$
19. $\dfrac{1}{3}$
20. $\dfrac{4}{8}$
21. $\dfrac{4}{8}$
22. $\dfrac{4}{5}$
23. $\dfrac{1}{9}$
24. $\dfrac{4}{11}$
25. $\dfrac{6}{8}$
26. $\dfrac{2}{6}$
27. $\dfrac{3}{4}$
28. $\dfrac{3}{6}$
29. $\dfrac{1}{7}$
30. $\dfrac{3}{10}$
31. $\dfrac{5}{10}$
32. $\dfrac{2}{5}$
33. $\dfrac{3}{12}$
34. $\dfrac{11}{12}$
35. $\dfrac{5}{9}$
36. $\dfrac{7}{9}$
37. $\dfrac{4}{7}$
38. $\dfrac{10}{12}$
39. $\dfrac{1}{4}$
40. $\dfrac{1}{11}$

Set 2

1. $\dfrac{8}{10}$
2. $\dfrac{7}{10}$
3. $\dfrac{3}{8}$
4. $\dfrac{7}{12}$
5. $\dfrac{2}{5}$

6. $\dfrac{2}{6}$
7. $\dfrac{5}{6}$
8. $\dfrac{1}{3}$
9. $\dfrac{3}{4}$
10. $\dfrac{4}{9}$

11. $\dfrac{5}{9}$
12. $\dfrac{3}{6}$
13. $\dfrac{6}{11}$
14. $\dfrac{9}{12}$
15. $\dfrac{4}{11}$

16. $\dfrac{1}{12}$
17. $\dfrac{2}{9}$
18. $\dfrac{7}{11}$
19. $\dfrac{2}{10}$
20. $\dfrac{11}{12}$

21. $\dfrac{1}{12}$
22. $\dfrac{2}{5}$
23. $\dfrac{5}{7}$
24. $\dfrac{3}{6}$
25. $\dfrac{3}{11}$

26. $\dfrac{2}{4}$
27. $\dfrac{9}{10}$
28. $\dfrac{3}{12}$
29. $\dfrac{1}{7}$
30. $\dfrac{9}{11}$

31. $\dfrac{2}{3}$
32. $\dfrac{4}{11}$
33. $\dfrac{3}{4}$
34. $\dfrac{4}{7}$
35. $\dfrac{4}{8}$

36. $\dfrac{8}{9}$
37. $\dfrac{3}{5}$
38. $\dfrac{5}{11}$
39. $\dfrac{5}{9}$
40. $\dfrac{4}{9}$

Set 3

1.
2.
3.
4.
5.

6.
7.
8.
9.
10.

11.
12.
13.
14.
15.

16.
17.
18.
19.
20.

21.
22.
23.
24.
25.

26.
27.
28.
29.
30.

31.
32.
33.
34.
35.

36.
37.
38.
39.
40.

Set 4

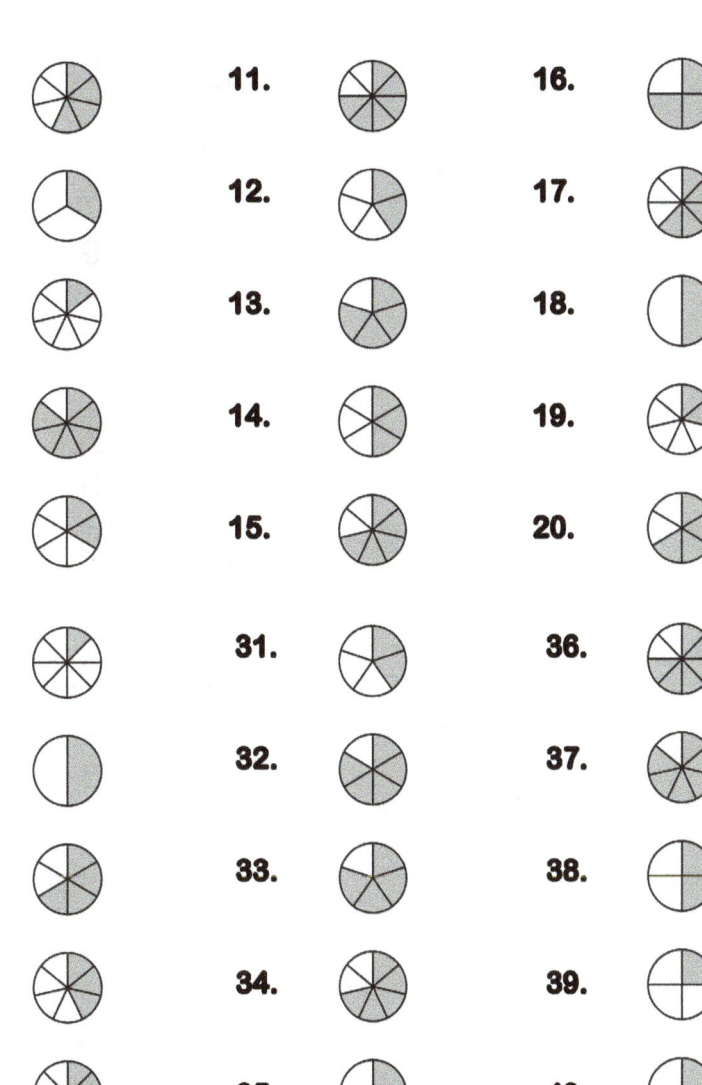

Set 5

1. $\dfrac{5}{6}$
2. $\dfrac{11}{12}$
3. $\dfrac{10}{11}$
4. $\dfrac{6}{7}$
5. $\dfrac{2}{3}$
6. $\dfrac{3}{5}$
7. $\dfrac{9}{11}$
8. $\dfrac{6}{9}$
9. $\dfrac{9}{10}$
10. $\dfrac{8}{12}$
11. $\dfrac{9}{12}$
12. $\dfrac{5}{9}$
13. $\dfrac{3}{4}$
14. $\dfrac{4}{8}$
15. $\dfrac{2}{4}$
16. $\dfrac{6}{9}$
17. $\dfrac{10}{11}$
18. $\dfrac{2}{3}$
19. $\dfrac{5}{12}$
20. $\dfrac{5}{8}$
21. $\dfrac{3}{6}$
22. $\dfrac{3}{5}$
23. $\dfrac{8}{10}$
24. $\dfrac{8}{9}$
25. $\dfrac{7}{11}$
26. $\dfrac{10}{12}$
27. $\dfrac{4}{10}$
28. $\dfrac{5}{12}$

29. $\dfrac{4}{6}$

30. $\dfrac{5}{10}$

31. $\dfrac{6}{7}$

32. $\dfrac{3}{10}$

33. $\dfrac{9}{12}$

34. $\dfrac{10}{12}$

35. $\dfrac{2}{5}$

36. $\dfrac{7}{12}$

37. $\dfrac{3}{4}$

38. $\dfrac{8}{9}$

39. $\dfrac{8}{11}$

40. $\dfrac{7}{9}$

41. $\dfrac{2}{3}$

42. $\dfrac{9}{11}$

43. $\dfrac{7}{10}$

44. $\dfrac{6}{11}$

45. $\dfrac{4}{9}$

46. $\dfrac{4}{6}$

47. $\dfrac{3}{12}$

48. $\dfrac{2}{3}$

49. $\dfrac{10}{11}$

50. $\dfrac{2}{4}$

51. $\dfrac{6}{7}$

52. $\dfrac{7}{9}$

53. $\dfrac{10}{12}$

54. $\dfrac{6}{12}$

55. $\dfrac{2}{10}$

56. $\dfrac{2}{5}$

www.ingramcontent.com/pod-product-compliance
Lightning Source LLC
LaVergne TN
LVHW061322060426
835507LV00019B/2264